The Quick Sketch Collection

# Short Change

## Stephen Deal

NIMBUS
Press

# Acknowledgements

We would like to thank Kingsway Publications, Lottbridge Drove, Eastbourne, for giving us permission to use the following material : 'Would you Adam and Eve it?', 'Short Change', 'The Cost of Living', 'Witness for the Prosecution', 'Thieves Paradise', 'Stephen' and 'Spies R Us' all originally published in *Burning Questions* (Eastbourne, 1993).

We would also like to thank The Bible Society, Stonehill Green, Westlea, Swindon, for allowing us to use 'The Five Minute Bible' and 'The Book of Fish', both originally published in *Entertaining Angels* (1998).

Scripture quotations taken from the HOLY BIBLE, NEW INTERNATIONAL VERSION. Copyright c 1973, 1978, 1984 by International Bible Soceity. Used by permission of Hodder & Stoughton Limited. All rights reserved. "NIV" is a registered trademark of International Bible Society. UK trademark number 1448790.

Published by Nimbus Press,
18 Guilford Road, Leicester, LE2 2RB.
Tel. 0116 270 6318
Web site: http://www.nimbuspress.co.uk
Email: publisher@nimbuspress.co.uk

*Cover illustration by Polly Deal*

British Library Cataloguing in Publication
Data available

ISBN 1 874424 67 5

Printed in Great Britain by
Cambrian Printers, Llanbadarn Road, Aberystwyth, SY23 3TN

For Matthew Tudor Deal

# Introduction

Thank you for buying (or at least browsing) this, the third in the Quick Sketch Collection series.

I am sometimes asked to lead what are usually labelled 'Creative Writing' workshops or seminars. I normally dread these occasions right up to the moment the session starts. But then, invariably I find myself thoroughly enjoying the experience. I dread the sessions because I am generally at a loss as to how to communicate the idea of creativity, especially within a Christian context.

There are some, and I suspect if you have attended a church for long enough you have met them, who are regularly blessed by receiving poems, sketches or stories straight from the Lord. You get the impression that they place a blank notebook under their pillow at night and come the morning it is filled with revelatory prose.

The trouble is, it doesn't work this way for most of us. I can't tell you the number of times I've stared at a blank computer screen and tried to will words onto it. No matter how many times I adjust the font size or fiddle with the page layout the screen remains resolutely blank. It is not until I grudgingly (and after much procrastination) actually start typing, deleting, retyping and pushing words around the screen that things begin to happen. Surely that's obvious you say, and you, being wise and astute, would be right. But you'd be amazed at the number of people for whom it is not so obvious.

Back to the 'Creative Writing' workshops for a moment. At some point during the session someone will tell me they have a brilliant idea for a play or sketch or whatever. They expound enthusiastically on their idea and I nod encouragingly. The idea may be complete rubbish but more often than not it is a genuinely good and original idea. The only thing stopping it actually being something truly creative is the fact that they have yet to get around to writing it. They ask me how I came to be a writer and I tell them I started to write things down. I have no idea whether they have the potential to be a good writer or not but unless they move from thinking about ideas to putting them down on paper (or, as is more likely these days, hard disk) neither they, nor we, will ever know.

I hope you find the sketches contained within this slim (though remarkably reasonably priced) volume useful or at least mildly amusing. None of them were dictated directly to me by the Lord. All of them were at some point just ideas waiting to happen. This book is physical proof that you don't have to receive inspiration from God via burning bushes or writing on banquet room walls – sometimes you just have to simply get on with writing your own ideas down. The point being that there's nothing super-spiritual about writing sketches (or plays, poems, songs etc). We all have the potential for creativity to some extent or another.

The reason why I always enjoy the 'Creative Writing' workshops I run in the end is that there is always someone there with an idea I would never have thought of in a million years. They make me laugh or think or both. I hope one or more of the pieces in this collection will make you do likewise. Better yet, I hope they encourage you to have a go at putting whatever God-given creative potential you have into practice.

Stephen Deal, 2002.

## Performance and Copyright

# Contents

# Stable Relationships

## Characters

*Ruth*

*Jacob*

## Bible Background

*Matthew 2.1-12*

*On stage is a typical nativity scene. Mary and Joseph with the baby Jesus are greeting the three wise men. Off to one side are the innkeeper (Jacob) and his wife (Ruth).*

*It should be possible to perform this sketch without actually seeing the nativity scene if you do not have enough people in your cast.*

**Ruth**      Well who are they?

**Jacob**     They say they are three kings from somewhere called Orient R.

**Ruth**      I've never heard of it.

**Jacob**     And they say they are very wise.

**Ruth**      Then what are they doing in our stable? Are they lost?

**Jacob**     No my little pumpkin, they've been following that star.

**Ruth**      What star?

**Jacob**     The one you've been complaining about these past few weeks. The one you say is so bright it has been giving you migraines.

**Ruth**      Oh, that star. If these gentlemen have anything to do with that star you just tell them to take it away and let it shine over someone else's stable keeping them awake at night. I won't have it any longer. It's been attracting all sorts of unsuitable people to the area.

**Jacob**     Like whom, petal?

**Ruth**    Like those shepherds who rolled in here during the middle of the night shouting about angelic hosts and tide marks of great joy. I'd only just gotten off to sleep as well.

**Jacob**    There has been a lot going on just recently.

**Ruth**    And it's all to do with those two and that poor, poor baby.

**Jacob**    They certainly do seem to be at the centre of things, my love.

**Ruth**    It's the little one I feel sorry for. What chance in life has he got? Look at his parents, they're as poor as synagogue mice.

**Jacob**    But they seem very happy as a family. You can see they love the child.

**Ruth**    Yes, but sometimes love is not enough. What sort of future has he got?

**Jacob**    Well if those three royal gentlemen are anything to go by, a pretty good one I should think. Perhaps he'll end up as a King himself.

**Ruth**    Don't be silly, Kings aren't born in stables, only poor people are.

**Jacob**    Look, they're giving the baby some presents.

**Ruth**    You can never have enough booties, that's what I say.

*The three kings give Mary and Joseph the three gifts.*

**Jacob**    *(To Mary and Joseph)* Let me give you a hand with those. You don't want to get hay all over them.

*The innkeeper takes the gifts and puts them somewhere in view of the audience. His wife investigates them.*

**Ruth**    Let me see ... Gold, incense, and myrrh. Oh very nice. Very nice, but not very practical. A couple of knitted romper suits would be of more immediate use.

**Jacob**   People like to be symbolic on occasions like these, my treasure. They like to give something that will last.

**Ruth**    Perhaps you are right. These gifts are about the only thing that will last. I don't give this family much chance. The rumour is that they've only been married a few months, if you take my meaning. It's all very sad really.

**Jacob**   Oh I don't know. Look at the mother. Whatever her problems may have been, she looks very contented now. The way she holds the child, you can tell that he's always going to be loved by someone. There's something special there.

**Ruth**    I'm just glad that our children weren't born in such squalid conditions.

**Jacob**   I don't suppose they would have chosen our stable either.

*The three wise men start to exit.*

**Jacob**   *(To the backs of the departing Kings)* Are you off then? It was nice meeting you. If you are ever passing this way again and need somewhere to stay, you just call on us.

**Ruth**    Very reasonable rates.

**Jacob**   'Bye then.

**Ruth**    'Bye. What charming gentlemen. They are exactly the kind of guests we ought to be trying to attract to our establishment now.

**Jacob**   Why now?

**Ruth**    Now we're a one star hotel of course.

### END

# Poor Value

## Characters
*Vicar puppet*
*Henry (rich puppet)*
*Ruth (poor puppet)*

## Bible Background
*Mark 12.41-44*

*In this sketch for puppets the vicar puppet is in the pulpit. Elsewhere a large collection box stands clearly in view. The Ruth and Henry puppets wait behind a screen then pop up into view.*

**Vicar**   *(Muttering)* Now where was I? Oh yes! We've got to have a reading from the … the … whatdayacallit? Um, book. Lots of stories. You know, Moses, Noah, Sampson. That lot. The Bible! That's it! The new bit. The part with Jesus. Where are my notes? Ah yes.

*(Reading)* Today's reading is taken from the gospel of Mark, chapter twelve and verses forty-one to forty-four.

Ahem! "Jesus sat down opposite the place where the offerings were put and watched the crowd putting their money into the temple treasury. Many rich people threw in large amounts."

*Enter Henry. He clutches a large wad of cash. Enter Ruth clutching a purse and carrying a bag.*

**Henry**   *(Singing)* Money, money, money, in a rich man's world. Now let me see; shall I drive the Porsche or take the train?

**Ruth**   Should I take the bus or should I walk?

**Henry**   I think I'll take the train. That way I can play with my lap-top and smirk at the passengers in second class.

**Ruth**   If I take the bus, I can do my knitting.

| | |
|---|---|
| **Henry** | *(Noticing the audience)* What are you lot looking at? Haven't you ever seen a rich puppet before? |
| **Ruth** | *(Also noticing the audience)* Oh hello. Don't mind me, I'm just on my way home. But there's something I've got to do first. |
| **Henry** | *(To audience)* I expect you're wondering just how rich I am. Well, compared to me, Basil Brush is a pauper. And as for that Thunderbirds crowd, I could buy Tracey Island three times over. |
| **Ruth** | *(To Henry)* Excuse me Sir. |
| **Henry** | What? |
| **Ruth** | Excuse me Sir, I need to get past. |
| **Henry** | What's that got to do with me? |
| **Ruth** | I'm afraid you're in my way. |
| **Henry** | Then you'll just have to wait. I'm telling these people here just how rich I am. |
| **Ruth** | Will that take long? |
| **Henry** | Well, since I'm very, very rich indeed it may take a very, very long time. |
| **Ruth** | Oh dear. |
| **Henry** | Anyway, why are you in such a hurry? |
| **Ruth** | I have to do something before I catch my bus. |
| **Henry** | You have something to do before you catch your bus? What, pray, could be so important as to be worth interrupting a very wealthy puppet like myself? |
| **Ruth** | I'm going to make my offering at the temple. |
| **Henry** | What? You are going to put money into that collection box over there? |

| | |
|---|---|
| **Ruth** | Yes. |
| **Henry** | But why would you want to? You're poor aren't you? |
| **Ruth** | The money goes to do God's work. I want to help. |
| **Henry** | And you've got enough money have you? |
| **Ruth** | Well … |
| **Henry** | *(Loudly)* Stand aside everyone – rich puppet walking. |

*Henry moves towards the collection box.*

| | |
|---|---|
| **Ruth** | What are you doing? |
| **Henry** | I'm going to put some money in the collection box. Now, let me see. How much should I give? |
| **Ruth** | I don't know. |
| **Henry** | *(Holding up his wad of cash)* Look everybody! I'm going to put lots of money into the box. Please take note – I, Henry Fforbes Smythe Robinson am putting in lots and lots of dosh. See what a good chap I am. |

*Henry puts the money in the box.*

| | |
|---|---|
| **Vicar** | Ahem! |
| **Henry** | What? |
| **Vicar** | If I may continue with the bible reading? |
| **Henry** | Oh, go on then. |
| **Vicar** | As I was saying. "Many rich people threw in large amounts." |
| **Henry** | That's me! I've just done that. I'm in the Bible. It must be because I'm so rich. |
| **Vicar** | *(Reading)* "But a poor widow came and put in two very small copper coins worth only a fraction of a penny." |
| **Henry** | A fraction of a penny! Ha! I put in loads. |

| | |
|---|---|
| **Ruth** | Excuse me. *(Ruth moves to the box and looks in her purse.)* |
| **Henry** | Come on, come on. What are you waiting for? |
| **Ruth** | Oh dear, I've only got a tiny amount of money. |
| **Henry** | Not like me. |
| **Ruth** | All I've got is my bus fare home. Well, never mind. It won't hurt me to walk. *(Ruth drops her money into the box}* |
| **Henry** | Is that all? God's not going to be too chuffed with you, is he? Not after he sees how much I put in. |
| **Vicar** | *(Reading)* Ahem! "Calling his disciples to him, Jesus said, "I tell you the truth. This poor widow has put more into the treasury than all the others. They all gave out of their wealth; but she, out of her poverty, put in everything – all she had to live on." |
| **Henry** | What! Now wait a cotton pickin' minute! Are you saying this old woman gave more than I did? |
| **Vicar** | In God's eyes she did. |
| **Henry** | But she's barely one step up from a sock puppet. How can anything she do be better than what I do? I'm rich, I'm famous, I'm ... I'm fantastic! |
| **Vicar** | You heard Jesus. She gave everything she has but you only gave a tiny part of your wealth. |
| **Henry** | I don't believe it! It's absurd. What kind of world would it be if the poor were more important than the rich? |
| **Vicar** | Heaven? |

*Ruth and Henry start to exit together.*

| | |
|---|---|
| **Ruth** | *(To Henry)* Come along dear, you've had a bit of a shock. You need a nice strong cup of tea. |
| **Henry** | And a biscuit? |

**Ruth**    If you like.

**Henry**    A Jammy Dodger? I like them.

*They exit*

**Vicar**    Well, well, well. You see, God's view of the world is different to ours. It's all a bit topsy-turvy. It doesn't matter to him how rich or poor you are on the outside – it's what's in your heart that matters.

Now, did someone mention a cup of tea and a Jammy Dodger?

## END

# Head in the Clouds

## Characters
*Cloud*
*Susan*

## Bible Background
*Matthew 5.3*

*Cloud, a hippyish looking man, stands behind the counter in a New Age shop. He wears beads and sunglasses.*

*Enter Susan.*

**Cloud**    Like, welcome, seeker after truth.

**Susan**    Actually, my name's Susan.

**Cloud**    Cosmic. I'm Cloud Walker.

**Susan**    You must have had a really tough time at school.

**Cloud**    How may this humble servant of the Universal Oneness bring enlightenment to you?

**Susan**    Pardon?

**Cloud**    How can I, like, help you?

**Susan**    I don't know if you can. I'm looking for something.

**Cloud**    Then you've come to the right place. This shop is a nexus for the spiritual forces of the New Age. If your chi is misaligned, you can harmonise your yin and yang here.

**Susan**    Weren't they a couple of pandas at London Zoo?

**Cloud**    Many seekers wish to re-energise their chakras, the mystical energy centres of the body.

**Susan**    Do they?

**Cloud**    They feel drained by today's materialistic, consumer led society.

| | |
|---|---|
| **Susan** | I have been feeling a bit drained recently. |
| **Cloud** | Then perhaps you need to Feng Shui your environment. |
| **Susan** | Isn't that where someone comes and rearranges your furniture? |
| **Cloud** | That right. They align your home with the currents of the cosmic breath. |
| **Susan** | I don't know. My mum had her flat Feng Shuied. They aligned her television and video recorder with the living room window. |
| **Cloud** | And did it change her fortunes? |
| **Susan** | You could say that. The next day she was burgled. |
| **Cloud** | Oh, bad karma. |
| **Susan** | Have you got anything to stop me feeling so empty? I feel as though something is missing. |
| **Cloud** | May I examine your aura? |
| **Susan** | I suppose so. |

*Cloud looks her up and down.*

| | |
|---|---|
| **Cloud** | Wow! I see darkness all around you. |
| **Susan** | Perhaps you should take off your sunglasses. |
| **Cloud** | Oh yeah. |

*Cloud removes the sunglasses.*

| | |
|---|---|
| **Susan** | Now what do you see? |
| **Cloud** | I see a red glow all around you. |
| **Susan** | What does that mean? |
| **Cloud** | It means you have a fiery personality. |
| **Susan** | Oh. |
| **Cloud** | Or it could mean you had Reddy-Brek for breakfast. Sometimes the psychic meanings are unclear. I wish my auntie were here. |

| | |
|---|---|
| **Susan** | Why? |
| **Cloud** | She had a psychic gift. I used to help her out a lot. |
| **Susan** | *(Gleefully)* You mean you were a psychic's sidekick? |
| **Cloud** | Yeah. |
| **Susan** | I've always been puzzled by something. |
| **Cloud** | What? |
| **Susan** | Why do psychics have to ask your name? |
| **Cloud** | Deep. |
| **Susan** | What did your auntie do? |
| **Cloud** | She used clairvoyance to see the future. |
| **Susan** | Was she any good? |
| **Cloud** | Yeah. She said I'd have a beautiful girlfriend. |
| **Susan** | And did you? |
| **Cloud** | I don't know. She also said she'd leave me before we met. |
| **Susan** | Look, do you have something to help me or not? |
| **Cloud** | How about Astrology? |
| **Susan** | You mean Horoscopes and star signs? |
| **Cloud** | It's based on ancient scientific principles. Using the wisdom of the ancients, I'd guess you are Leo with Taurus rising in the house of Capricorn. |
| **Susan** | Actually, I'm Visa with debts rising in the House of Fraser. |
| **Cloud** | Heavy. We could try looking in my auntie's crystal ball. |
| **Susan** | How does it work? |
| **Cloud** | My auntie would take it in her hands and gently shake it. |
| **Susan** | What would she foresee? |

| | |
|---|---|
| **Cloud** | A snow storm usually. |
| **Susan** | I don't know; we don't seem to be getting anywhere. I want something that meets my spiritual needs. I'm comfortably off, I've got a nice family, nice friends, a good job, and a pleasant home, but my life seems to be missing something. |
| **Cloud** | "Blessed are the poor in spirit for theirs is the kingdom of Heaven." |
| **Susan** | Pardon? |
| **Cloud** | It's just something my Granny used to say. It's from the Bible I think. |
| **Susan** | What does it mean? |
| **Cloud** | I think it means you're blessed if you realise there's something spiritual missing in your life. I suppose most people are too busy to notice. |
| **Susan** | Well I've noticed. |
| **Cloud** | It's what the New Age is all about. It provides instant spiritual solutions for people with busy lives. |
| **Susan** | A sort of mystical pick 'n' mix. |
| **Cloud** | You pick the psychic remedy that best meets your needs of the moment. If you're concerned for the future, the answers are in the stars or the tarot or the runes. |
| **Susan** | I see. |
| **Cloud** | If you're concerned about health then you can turn to crystals, homeopathy or psychic surgeons. |
| **Susan** | Right. |
| **Cloud** | And if you're concerned about reaching your full potential you can practice astral projection, dianetics or eastern mysticism. |
| **Susan** | What about Christianity? |

18

| | |
|---|---|
| **Cloud** | Christianity? No, that's way too old-fashioned. |
| **Susan** | I thought the New Age was all about ancient forms of spiritual truth. |
| **Cloud** | Well yes, but you have to draw a line somewhere. |
| **Susan** | I don't understand. |
| **Cloud** | The whole Jesus thing is so yesterday. I mean the dude died and that's so negative, right? |
| **Susan** | But he died because he said all these radical things, didn't he? |
| **Cloud** | Exactly! What's the point of getting killed for your beliefs? You just have to modify them a bit, write a book and then run a two-week residential course to empower your followers. |
| **Susan** | So, it's all right to be spiritually poor so long as you're materially rich enough to buy self-help videos and one-to-one counselling sessions with your personal guru. |
| **Cloud** | But isn't that what people want? Neatly packaged answers to life's great mysteries? |
| **Susan** | It just seems so cynical. |
| **Cloud** | It's modern. |
| **Susan** | I don't care. I don't believe the answers to life's problems are in the cards or written in the stars. |
| **Cloud** | Well surely you don't think they can be found nailed to a cross? |
| **Susan** | I don't know – maybe they can. Anyway, I didn't come here to debate religion; I came to buy a present for my boyfriend. Any ideas? |
| **Cloud** | How about one of these? |

*Cloud reaches behind the counter and brings out a ludicrous looking hat made out of twigs and dripping with crystals.*

| | |
|---|---|
| **Susan** | What is it? |

**Cloud**      It's a traditional Old English pagan dream-catcher. You wear it in bed and it protects you from bad karma.

**Susan**      I'm not sure. Don't you think he'd feel a bit silly?

*Cloud puts it on his head.*

**Cloud**      Oh no, you can trust me on this. In a previous life, I used to be a fashion designer. *(Cloud strikes a pose.)*

## END

# Mourning Has Broken

## Characters
*Beverly*
*David*

## Bible Background
*Matthew 5.4*

*Beverly sits at a desk in the reception area for the Kingdom of Heaven. She has a computer before her. Enter David, clutching an electric drill. His hair stands on end and his clothes are burnt.*

**Beverly**   Hello and welcome to the Kingdom of Heaven. My name is Beverly. How may I be of assistance?

**David**   I'm not sure but I think there's been a terrible mistake.

**Beverly**   I see. And exactly what is the nature of the mistake?

**David**   I don't think I should be here.

**Beverly**   Oh don't worry Sir, lots of people don't feel worthy of entry into the Kingdom of Heaven.

**David**   No, it's not that.

**Beverly**   Then why don't you think you should be here?

**David**   I'm not dead.

**Beverly**   Hmm, let me check our records. May I have your name?

**David**   David Thomas.

*Beverly refers to the computer.*

**Beverly**   David Thomas … would that be the David Thomas previously of 27 Acadia avenue?

**David**   What do you mean *previously*?

**Beverly**   According to our computer, you are dead.

| | |
|---|---|
| **David** | And which are you going to believe, the evidence of your own eyes or your computer? |
| **Beverly** | Don't be silly – the computer. |
| **David** | But I can't be dead. I haven't been ill or anything. |
| **Beverly** | What's the last thing you remember before coming here? |
| **David** | It's a bit hazy but I remember trying to fix the TV aerial with my power drill. |
| **Beverly** | Would that have been up on your roof? |
| **David** | That's right. |
| **Beverly** | During a thunderstorm? |
| **David** | Yes, the lightning was playing havoc with the picture. |
| **Beverly** | Was there a bright flash and the sudden smell of burning? |
| **David** | How did you know? |
| **Beverly** | Just a wild guess. |
| **David** | I'm dead aren't I? |
| **Beverly** | Yes. |
| **David** | And this is heaven. |
| **Beverly** | Technically, it's just outside heaven. The pearly gates are just down there on your right. |
| **David** | And Saint Peter is waiting there to greet me? |
| **Beverly** | Oh no, he's much too busy. I'm afraid he only has time for the important people. |
| **David** | What, like Prime Ministers and film stars? |
| **Beverly** | Hardly. He only has time for the people who really matter, like that lady over there. |
| **David** | Who, the one in the hospital gown? |

**Beverly**    She's just spent seventeen hours on a hospital trolley. They haven't even noticed she's gone yet.

**David**    Has anyone noticed I've gone?

*Beverly briefly checks her computer.*

**Beverly**    Oh yes. And they've noticed that the reception on Channel Five has improved.

**David**    They must be devastated.

**Beverly**    Yes, there's very little on worth watching. Oh, sorry, I see what you mean. Yes, I'm afraid they're very upset.

**David**    Isn't there anything I can do?

**Beverly**    Like what?

**David**    I don't know; write them a note to tell them I'm all right.

**Beverly**    Oh no, that's not allowed.

**David**    But I want them to take comfort that I'm in a better place.

**Beverly**    Oh don't worry. That message has already been sent.

**David**    It has?

**Beverly**    The redeemer has told everybody that "blessed are those who mourn, for they shall be comforted."

### END

# Jonah
## Characters
*Jonah*

## Bible Background
*The book of Jonah*

*Lights up on Jonah, sitting under a tree, mending a sandal.*

My name is Jonah. Yes, that Jonah. The "swallowed by a big fish" Jonah ... the "I bet he had a whale of a time" Jonah. Very funny. Ha, ha. Do you see me laughing? Do you think I like being the joke of the Bible? You hear them say ... "and the story of Jonah just goes to show that you can't run away from God". Then everyone closes their Bible and says, "silly old Jonah. If only he'd done what he'd been told, life would have been so much easier!"

Well, it wasn't that simple. There I was, sat at home making sandals ... Oh, and keeping one eye on my father, Amitti, who's getting on a bit and tends to wander off and buy camels if you let him, when suddenly, the word of the Lord comes to me. No real problem there ... except that I managed to sew a piece of leather to my thumb in surprise ...

"Jonah," the voice said, "Jonah."

"I heard you the first time!" I said.

"Don't get touchy," said the voice, "I've got a job for you."

Well, I had a look to see if anyone was having a joke at Jonah's expense, found that Amitti had slipped away to buy camel food, so I was totally alone ...

"Jonah," said the voice again, "don't waste my time, there's work to be done."

"You want some sandals mended?" I asked.

"Don't be facetious," says the Lord, "I want you to go to Nineveh and preach against its wickedness."

"You've got to be joking, O' Lord," I replied. "The people of Nineveh are vicious. You know the tortures they inflict on their enemies? I can't go there."

"Want to bet?" said the Lord.

Well, you know what happened next. I very sensibly hopped on the first boat going to Tarshish - which was about as far away from Nineveh as you can get. No way was I going to that hell hole. Anyway, I was asleep downstairs, sorry, 'below decks', when the Lord blew up this terrific storm, and it looks as though the boat I'm on is going to sink. The sailors start to throw the cargo overboard, in an attempt to lighten the ship, but to no avail. Then they start praying to their gods ... still nothing happens. Eventually the Captain comes down and wakes me up.

Now notice that I said, 'wakes me up' ... because I'm still asleep. During a raging storm, I, Jonah, am asleep! Why am I asleep? Because I have a clear conscience, that's why. Because I did not feel guilty about not going to Nineveh. Because I knew I was doing the right thing, in disobeying God.

Well, the Captain says to me,

"Get up and pray to your God. Maybe he will hear your prayer and have mercy on us."

Meanwhile, the crew has been drawing lots to decide whose fault the situation is. Guess who copped the short straw! I told them it was God's fault, for being angry with me for not doing what he wanted ... I also told them the best way out of the mess was to throw me overboard. Well, it was me God wanted, not them, and the sooner I was off the ship, the sooner he would leave them alone.

So they had to bung me into the briny deep, and straight away the sea goes calm, but by then it's too late. I'm in the water ... and since there's not much call for it in sandal making, I can't swim, so I'm drowning ... drowning and praying and shouting,

"Okay, okay Lord, you win. I think you're wrong, but I'll go. I just don't want to drown."

Now we get to the bit of the story that everybody thinks they know ... I was swallowed by a big fish.

"Jonah," people say to me, "Jonah, was it a fish, or was it a whale ... And if it was a whale, ... what kind?"

What a stupid question ... within half a second I was inside the thing ... what am I, a marine biologist that I can identify a fish from the design of its stomach? It was cold and wet and smelly. I said to the Lord,

"Oh, thanks a lot!"

And he says,

"What do you expect in the middle of the ocean at such short notice ... A first-class cabin with steward service? Now be serious Jonah, go to Nineveh and preach against its wickedness!"

Well, I didn't really have a lot of choice. It wasn't a pleasant journey. It was dark and cramped. There was plenty of food, but it was mostly second hand. Somehow I just didn't feel all that hungry. Instead I spent the next three days in fervent prayer.

Then suddenly - ugh! The fish, or whatever, vomits me up on this beach and the word of the Lord comes to me again and says,

"Now, go to the great city of Nineveh and proclaim to it the message I give you."

So off I went.

Now, Nineveh is a big city. Almost three days walk to cross it. And I had to go right to the centre with the message that in forty days time the city would be destroyed. I had no trouble getting the people to notice me. The acids in the fish's stomach had bleached my skin and my hair. I think the people took one look at me and said,

"Hey, his God scares him so much he's turned white!"

You bet they took notice!

So I preached God's message to them, and very soon the whole city had repented, and everyone was very happy. Well, everyone except me. I was so mad I could spit!

Now we get to the part of my story that really puzzles people - why was I mad at the Lord?

The reason I was mad at God was because I knew that when the Ninevites repented he would have mercy on them and forgive them. And that seemed unjust to me. The Ninevites were scum. They were evil in every sense of the word. They hurled their enemies down on to spikes in pits. They killed women and children ... by torture. I felt so angry!

The trouble with God is that he is very difficult to be mad at. What do you do? Throw stones at him? Scream and shout? Me? I sulked. He had used me to do something I did not want to do. What did he expect, a cheery wave and a shout of "anytime!?" I felt messed about. Then God said to me,

"Nineveh has more than one hundred and twenty thousand people who cannot tell their right arm from their left. Should I not be concerned with that great city?"

What could I say? I said nothing. If God chooses to forgive anyone, who am I, a sandal-maker, to argue? I still feel uncomfortable that his forgiveness extends to those I would consider unforgivable ... but he is the Lord, and I am his servant.

When I got back home, I had another mess to sort out. In my enforced absence, my dotty old father had managed to buy thirty-seven camels. Oi! No wonder I've got the hump!

*Lights begin to fade.*

Well, what do you expect? Humour from a man who spends his time in the belly of a fish?

*Blackout.*

**END**

# Try me a River

## Characters
*Joshua*
*3 Soldiers*

## Bible Background
*Joshua 1.1-11, 3.1-17*

*Joshua, son of Nun, addresses some of the soldiers in the army of the children of Israel. The soldiers all carry spears.*

**Joshua**    Okay chaps, at ease. It's absolutely splendid to see you all.

**Soldier 1**    Thank you Sir.

**Joshua**    So, are we all fighting fit?

**Soldier 2**    Yes Sir.

**Joshua**    So, we'd better get on with the task in hand.

**Soldier 3**    One question Sir?

**Joshua**    Yes?

**Soldier 3**    What task would that be?

**Joshua**    Oh right, silly of me not to have mentioned it.

**Soldier 2**    If you say so, Sir.

**Joshua**    We're to cross over the Jordan river and occupy the lands on the far side.

**Soldier 1**    One other question Sir?

**Joshua**    Fire away.

**Soldier 3**    Who are you Sir?

**Joshua**    Didn't I say?

**Soldier 1**    No Sir.

| | |
|---|---|
| **Joshua** | Gosh, how jolly rude of me. My name is Joshua, son of Nun. I'm the new Commander-in-Chief. |
| **Soldier 3** | What happened to the old one? The guy with the beard and those stone tablets we've been lugging about for forty years? Old what's-his-name? |
| **Soldier 1** | Moses. |
| **Soldier 3** | That's the geezer. Lovely bloke. Did that great trick with water. Wonderful man. I'd follow him to the ends of the earth, and round a desert for four decades. |
| **Joshua** | He died. |
| **Soldier 3** | He didn't did he? Why didn't anybody tell me? |
| **Joshua** | We have been mourning him for the last thirty days. Didn't you notice? |
| **Soldier 3** | I just thought people were fed up because it was manna for tea again. Ah no, that's terrible. I'm all upset now. |
| **Joshua** | I'm very sorry. If it's any consolation he died peacefully at the age of one hundred and twenty. |
| **Soldier 3** | So he had a good innings then. |
| **Joshua** | A very good innings. |
| **Soldier 3** | I'm pleased. So you're in charge now? |
| **Joshua** | Yes. If you don't mind, I'd like to get on with the business in hand. |
| **Soldier 2** | Which is? |
| **Joshua** | Crossing the Jordan and conquering all the territories from the desert to Lebanon, all the Hittite country, to the great sea on the west. Then from Gilead to Dan, all of Naphtali, the territory of Ephraim and Manasseh, all the land of Judah as far as the western sea, the Negev and the whole region from the valley of Jericho, as far as Zoar. |

**Soldier 2**   That's a whole lot of conquering.

**Joshua**   Yes it is.

**Soldier 2**   Conquer, conquer, conquer.

**Joshua**   The lord has promised to give us everywhere we put our feet. No one will be able to stand against us.

**Soldier 2**   Terrific.

**Joshua**   All we have to do is meditate upon the law and victory is assured. So long as we do not turn to the left nor to the right from it the land will be ours.

**Soldier 2**   I must say I like your style of leadership Sir. Moses had us carrying great big tabernacles around a desert for nearly half a century. You've only had the job five minutes and we've progressed from a nomadic tribe to an agrarian society of landowners almost overnight. Well done Sir.

**Joshua**   It's all the will of God.

**Soldier 1**   This law you mentioned …?

**Joshua**   The law handed down to us by Moses, yes?

**Soldier 1**   That would be the law with all the "thou shalt not do this" and "thou shalt not do that" and not eat anything that goeth "oink" or that would taste good in a thermidor sauce?

**Joshua**   That's not quite how I would have summarised it but, essentially, yes.

**Soldier 1**   Don't you think that's asking a bit much?

**Joshua**   What do you mean?

**Soldier 3**   Well, speaking for myself and the lads, we find quite a lot of the law a bit tricky to follow.

**Joshua**   Is that follow as in understand, or follow as in obey?

**All soldiers**Both.

**Joshua**    Let me see if I can help you. Over there we have a land of milk and honey, a land to call home, a land for our children to inherit, and all we have to do is obey God and follow the law.

**Soldier 3**    Right.

**Joshua**    And over here, and stop me if this is too difficult for you to understand, we have … *(He gestures)* some sand.

**Soldier 2**    A land of milk and honey versus a sandcastle.

**Joshua**    Precisely. Now if you don't have any further objections may we proceed with claiming our kingdom?

**Soldier 3**    Fine with me.

**Soldier 2**    And me.

**Soldier 1**    Count me in.

**Joshua**    Good. Okay troops – attention! *(The soldiers come to attention.)* Prepare to cross the Jordan river. Quick march. One, two, one, two, one, two. *(They all start to exit.)* To the river! Quick splash!

*The soldiers re-enter. They bring out inflatable flotation devices. (e.g. Rubber rings, arm bands.)*

### END

# Growing Pains

## Characters
*Narrators A & B*
*Some children*

## Bible Background
*Mark 4.1-20*

*Prepare two bamboo canes by tying lengths of string to them at regular intervals. Attach to the strings paper heads of corn and suitable leaves. Lie the canes across the front of the performing area. When they are lifted the effect should be of a line of corn growing up. You may need to weight the bottom of the strings.*

*The seeds sown in this sketch should be popcorn because it is easily seen and quickly picked up.*

*Narrators A and B stand to the left and right of the stage.*

**A**      A farmer went forth to sew.

**B**      And when he had finished hemming the curtains he went into his field to plant some seeds.

**A**      Like so.

*A farmer (A) starts sowing seeds. He throws them to the left and to the right. A and B hum the theme tune to the archers.*

**B**      We would like to draw your attention to our farmer's technique. This particular method of sowing seeds is called broadcasting.

**A**      Which is where the term comes from regarding radio and television.

**B**      We thought you'd like to know that.

**A**      In case you didn't already.

**B**      Some of the seeds fell upon the path.

**A**      Where they attracted the attention of a herd of birds.

**B**      A herd?

*A group of children rush in and grab the seeds, preferably with lots of 'tweets' and bird effects. After they have exited the farmer sows some more seeds.*

**A**      And some seeds fell on stony ground.

**B**      The corn grew up quickly.

*The first bamboo cane is lifted quickly.*

**A**      But the roots could not grow properly because of the stones and so the corn soon died.

*The bamboo cane is dropped. Everyone says "ahh"*

**B**      Other seeds grew up among weeds.

*The first bamboo cane is lifted again and people take up positions next to the corn.*

**A**      And the weeds throttled and strangled and mangled the corn.

*The people tear the corn apart, singing as they do so "'ere we go, 'ere we go, ere we go," in the manner of football supporters.*

**B**      But some of the seed fell upon good soil.

**A**      And grew to produce corn with as much as a hundred seeds each.

*The second bamboo cane is lifted and held as high as possible.*

**END**

# Talent less

## Characters

*Narrator / Rich man*
*Assistants: A,B & C*

## Bible Background

*Matthew 25.14-30*

**Narrator**  Once upon a time and in a far away land there lived a rich man.

**A**  A very rich man.

**B**  A very, very rich man.

**C**  A very, very, very rich man.

**Narrator**  Who was about to embark on a journey.

**A**  A very long journey.

**B**  A very, very long journey.

**C**  A very, very …

**Narrator**  *(Interrupting)* A journey of some considerable length. So he called together his most trusted servants.

   *A, B and C don't move.*

   He called together his most trusted servants. That's you three. Come 'ere.

   *A, B and C rush to the narrator and kneel at his feet.*

   That's better. And he addressed them thus. *(The narrator puts a crown on.)*

   Right chaps, I'm off on my hols. I'm going to be away for some time.

**A**  Have a nice time.

**B**  Send us a postcard.

| | |
|---|---|
| **Narrator** | But before I go I'm going to reward you for being such good servants. |
| **A** | Thank you, Sire. |
| **B** | You are most kind, your greatness. |
| **C** | Yippee! |
| **Narrator** | I'm going to entrust you to look after my fortune while I'm away. |
| **A, B & C** | Oh crumbs. |
| **Narrator** | *(The narrator removes the crown.)* The rich man gave each of the servants some money. To the first he gave five talents. |
| **A** | Wow! |
| **Narrator** | To the second he gave two talents. |
| **B** | Cor! |
| **Narrator** | And to the third he gave just one talent. |
| **C** | *(Insulted)* Huh! |
| **Narrator** | And then the man went on his journey. *(Puts crown on.)* Cheery bye. |
| **A, B & C** | Bye bye. |
| **Narrator** | *(Removes crown.)* And the servants set to work. The first servant took his five talents and invested the money. |
| **A** | *(Taking out a mobile phone.)* Hi, Nigel. Buy low, sell high. Buy! Sell! Buy! |
| **Narrator** | The second servant took his two talents and also put the money to work. |
| **B** | I'd like to open a high yield investment account please. |
| **Narrator** | *(To B.)* Certainly Sir. Here's your free backpack, pen and personal organiser. |

| | |
|---|---|
| **B** | Thank you. |
| **Narrator** | But the third servant took his one talent and dug a hole in the ground. |
| **C** | *(Miming digging.)* Dig – heave. Dig – heave. Dig – heave. |
| **Narrator** | And into the hole he dropped the coin. |
| **C** | *(Miming dropping the coin.)* Plink. |
| **Narrator** | After a long time the servants' master returned from his three week round the world holiday and two weeks caught up in a baggage handlers dispute at Paris airport and summoned his servants to him. |
| **A, B & C** | Here we are Sir. |
| **Narrator** | *(Putting crown on.)* Jolly good. Right chaps. How did we do with the talents I gave you? |
| **A** | I took my five talents and put them to work and gained five more. Now I have ten talents to return to you. |
| **Narrator** | Well done, good and faithful servant. You have been faithful with a few things; I will put you in charge of many things. Come and share your master's happiness. |
| **B** | I took my two talents and put them to work and gained two more.Now I have four talents to return to you. |
| **Narrator** | Well done, good and faithful servant. You have been faithful with a few things; I will put you in charge of many things. Come and share your master's happiness. |
| **C** | You know you gave me that talent to look after? |
| **Narrator** | Yes. |
| **C** | Well here it is. *(C holds out the coin to the narrator. The narrator refuses to take it.)* |
| **Narrator** | It's all muddy. |

| | |
|---|---|
| **C** | I can explain that. |
| **Narrator** | Go on. |
| **C** | I stuck it in a hole in the ground. |
| **Narrator** | Why? |
| **C** | I didn't want to lose it. |
| **Narrator** | Do you know who I am? |
| **C** | You are my master, master. |
| **Narrator** | And what kind of master am I? |
| **C** | Er … a very very nice one? |
| **Narrator** | No! I harvest where I have not sown and I gather where I have not scattered seed. I am one mean dude, dude. |
| **C** | I knew that. |
| **Narrator** | Then why were you so lazy? Why did you not work with what I gave you? You could have at least put it in the bank so it could have earned some interest. *(To B.)* Take the coin from this miserable servant and give it to the one who has ten talents. |
| **A** | Me! Me! |

*B takes the coin from C and gives it to A.*

| | |
|---|---|
| **B** | There you are. |
| **A** | Thanks. |
| **Narrator** | Now listen, when I give my servants something valuable I expect them to use it to bring riches to my kingdom - not to hide it away and waste the opportunity I have given them. |
| | For everyone who has will be given more and they shall have abundance. Whoever does not have, even what he has will be taken from him. |

Now throw that worthless worm out of my kingdom and into the darkness where he can wail and gnash his teeth.

*A and B bundle C off stage.*

C          *(As he exits.)* This seems a little harsh. Hang on, worms don't have teeth.

**Narrator**   Teeth will be provided!

## END

# Lilies in the Pink

**Characters**

*Daisy 1*

*Daisy 2*

*Lily*

**Bible Background**

*Matthew 6.25-34*

*Two Daisies stand either side of a Lily in a field.*

*Additional flowers can be played by actors or by the audience.*

**Daisy 1**  Morning, Daisy.

**Daisy 2**  Morning, Daisy.

**Daisy 1**  Ready?

**Daisy 2**  As I'll ever be.

**Daisy 1**  OK, let's stretch.

**Daisy 2**  Left, right, left, right, left, right. Come on; let's see that foliage.

*The whole field sways from left to right except for the Lily.*

**Daisy 1**  Okay, bend and up, bend and up. Push those petals.

*The whole field bends forward and back except for the Lily.*

**Daisy 2**  Excellent.

**Daisy 1**  *(Noticing Lily)* 'Ere, Daize, look at her.

**Daisy 2**  What's her game then?

**Daisy 1**  Dunno, Daize. *(To Lily)* 'Ere, what's your game?

*The Lily stretches languidly.*

**Daisy 2**  You ain't gonna get pretty just resting on your stalk.

**Daisy 1**  You've gotta work at it.

**Both**      Like us.

**Daisy 2**   Stretch, relax, stretch, and relax.

*The whole field except for Lily stretch and relax.*

**Daisy 1**   *(Looking at Lily)* I think she's a bit of a … you know …

**Daisy 2**   A half-hardy annual.

**Both**      Poor thing.

**Daisy 1**   'Ere, darling, what's your name?

*The Lily just stretches languidly.*

**Daisy 2**   I think she's a Lily.

**Daisy 1**   Oh … She looks very relaxed.

**Daisy 2**   Look at her – not a care in the world.

**Daisy 1**   Completely stress free.

**Daisy 2**   And here's us; getting our stamens in a tangle over every little thing.

**Daisy 1**   Slugs and snails.

**Daisy 2**   Frost and flooding.

**Daisy 1**   Cuckoo spit and Greenfly.

**Both**      Genetic Modification.

**Daisy 2**   But look at her.

**Daisy 1**   Dressed like royalty.

**Daisy 2**   It's as if she thinks there's a gardener looking after her.

**Daisy 1**   Ooh that would be nice; someone to rub baby-bio into your roots.

**Daisy 2**   Someone to give you a quick going over with the pruning shears.

**Daisy 1**   Someone to mulch your borders.

**Both**      Bliss.

**Daisy 1**   *(Addressing the field)* Okay girls. We've got a new regime.

**Daisy 2**   Do as the Lily does.

**Daisy 1**   One, two, three …

*The whole field stretches languidly.*

**All**       *(Blissfully)* Ahh …

**Daisy 2**   You know what I fancy, Daize?

**Daisy 1**   What?

**Daisy 2**   That Alan Titchmarsh as my personal trainer.

**Daisy 1**   He can pot my seedlings anytime.

**END**

# Would you Adam and Eve it?

## Characters

*Adam*

*Eve*

## Bible background

*Genesis 1-3*

*Adam and Eve stand behind a small shrub. They could wear a body suit or a simple white tea-shirt with fig-leaf attached symbolically. Or even shorts and braces have been worn!*

**Adam**  What's it all about? I ask you!

**Eve**  What are you whining on about now, Adam?

**Adam**  One moment we're in the Garden of Eden, paradise, the next, we're stuck out here and the whole place is covered in weeds. And all because of one stupid bit of fruit.

**Eve**  Oh don't bring that up again. I've said I'm sorry.

**Adam**  A whole blooming garden of fresh produce and you have to pick the one piece of forbidden vegetable matter. Why didn't you give me some passion fruit? I love passion fruit.

**Eve**  It wasn't my fault.

**Adam**  Oh yes. That's another thing. Why did you listen to a snake? A snake! I ask you. You never listen to me.

**Eve**  He was very persuasive.

**Adam**  He's a snake! How can a snake be persuasive?

**Eve**  Well he was so charming. He told me that if you and I ate the fruit of that particular tree we could gain wisdom.

**Adam**  And you believed him.

**Eve**  He seemed so wide-eyed and innocent.

| | |
|---|---|
| **Adam** | He's a snake, he hasn't got any eyelids. And if I ever get my hands on him he won't have any legs either. |
| **Eve** | Violence isn't the answer. |
| **Adam** | Oh yes? You tell that to the lion. He's just eaten three sheep. The whole worlds gone crazy I tell you. |
| **Eve** | It's not my fault. |
| **Adam** | Well it certainly isn't mine. I was perfectly happy pottering around doing a bit of pruning and naming the animals. |
| **Eve** | Well that's just the point isn't it. You were never there. But you expected me to get the supper. If you did your share of work around the house instead of leaving it all to me perhaps none of this would have happened. |
| **Adam** | Don't go shifting the blame on to me. I've been working flat out trying to find a name for that horse with the black and white stripes. |
| **Eve** | You'll have to start using another letter. |
| **Adam** | I've only got one left. Everything is running down and wearing out. |
| **Eve** | I know. This is the third set of fig leaves I've had to find this week. |
| **Adam** | I keep snagging mine on brambles and things. |
| **Eve** | Doesn't that hurt? |
| **Adam** | My eyes have been watering all day. I'm sick and tired of it all. Everything used to be so perfect but now it's all in shreds. |
| **Eve** | Quite literally I see. |
| **Adam** | Pick me another leaf will you. |
| **Eve** | Do it yourself, I'm not your servant. |
| **Adam** | You are so moody these days. |

| | |
|---|---|
| **Eve** | You leave my moods out of it. |
| **Adam** | I don't know what's got into you. |
| **Eve** | Men! |
| **Adam** | What do you mean men? There's only one of me. |
| **Eve** | Man then! |
| **Adam** | You know what I really want? I wish we could start all over again. |
| **Eve** | Well we can't. We have to pay the price for being disobedient. |
| **Adam** | We? |
| **Eve** | I'm sorry. I know you are going to blame me forever, but there's nothing we can do about it. |
| **Adam** | It's God I blame. He's the one who gave us free will and intelligence. He's the one who made us with the ability to mess up. He's the one who should find a way to make it all right again. |
| **Eve** | And how is he going to do that? |
| **Adam** | I don't know, but he should. Whatever it takes, whatever the cost. |
| **Eve** | Well there's no point whinging on. |
| **Adam** | I'm ravenous. How about roasting another unicorn? |
| **Eve** | No, we finished the last of those on Friday. There's some apple pie left. |
| **Adam** | No. I fancy something roasted. I wonder what that black and white horse tastes like? |

**END**

# Short Change

## Characters
*Beverly*
*Zacchaeus*

## Bible background
*Luke 19.1-10*

*This sketch takes place in the local branch of a bank. There is scope here for any number of non-speaking parts forming a queue behind Zacchaeus who pretends to fill out the various forms that Beverly gives him during the sketch.*

**Beverly**    Next please. Yes Sir, my name is Beverly, how may I be of assistance?

**Zacch.**    I'd like to withdraw some money.

**Beverly**    Certainly Sir, what name is it?

**Zacch.**    Zacchaeus.

**Beverly**    And do you have your account details?

**Zacch.**    No, I'm afraid I don't. I came out in rather a hurry.

**Beverly**    I'll have to ask you to fill out one of these green forms.

**Zacch.**    Fine.

**Beverly**    Which will authorise me to allow you to fill out a pink form.

**Zacch.**    Oh.

**Beverly**    And if you sign here, here, and here.

**Zacch.**    Right.

**Beverly**    And can you initial it to show me you've signed.

**Zacch.**    Er ... Right.

| | |
|---|---|
| **Beverly** | Now do you have any identification? |
| **Zacch.** | Not really. |
| **Beverly** | That presents me with a bit of a problem. You'll have to fill out an orange form. |
| **Zacch.** | Are we working our way through the rainbow? |
| **Beverly** | Oh very droll Sir. How much would you like to withdraw? |
| **Zacch.** | All of it. Every penny. |
| **Beverly** | I see. Going on holiday are we Sir? Anywhere nice? |
| **Zacch.** | No, I'm staying here in Jericho. |
| **Beverly** | Very wise. I get camel sick myself. Is Sir going to invest the money? |
| **Zacch.** | In a manner of speaking. I'm going to give to the poor and to the people I stole it from. |
| **Beverly** | Do they give a high rate of interest? |
| **Zacch.** | It's a long-term investment. |
| **Beverly** | How long? |
| **Zacch.** | Eternal. |
| **Beverly** | Lovely. Trying to avoid the taxman are you? |
| **Zacch.** | Not really. |
| **Beverly** | Not that I blame you. My local tax collector's really horrible. He looks a bit like you actually. |
| **Zacch.** | But a man can change can't he? He can start again. |
| **Beverly** | You sound just like that Jesus. He's been going around saying people can change and start all over again. Being born again he calls it. |
| **Zacch.** | Exactly. That's what he told me when he came to my house for tea. |

| Beverly | Jesus went to tea at your house, did he? Lovely. My mum went on a picnic with him. I hope you gave him more than bread and fish. |
|---|---|
| Zacch. | I gave him my life. *(Hands back the forms.)* |
| Beverly | Lovely. How do you want your money? |
| Zacch. | Cash please. |
| Beverly | *(She hands over a large sum of money.)* You be careful carrying this amount of money around with you. There are some very strange people about. |
| Zacch. | So I've noticed. |
| Beverly | Do you know what? My mum, yesterday morning, opened her bedroom curtains, and there was a man right outside the window. Sat up a tree he was.  Next please. |

**END**

# The Cost of Living

## Characters
*Dominic*
*Clarissa*
*Harris*
*Nanny*

## Bible background
Matthew 19.16-30

**Dominic**    Ah! My three closest friends. Thank you for coming so swiftly. Clarissa, my darling fiancée. Nanny, dear nanny. And Harris, my trusty manservant.

**Harris**    You rang, Sir?

**Dominic**    Indeed I did.

**Harris**    A matter of some import I would surmise.

**Dominic**    Absolutely! You would surmise correctly. I have some tremendous news.

**Clarissa**    Oh darling! Are we going to set the day?

**Nanny**    Congratulations Master Dominic.

**Dominic**    No, no, nothing like that. I've met someone.

**Clarissa**    Oh Dominic!

**Dominic**    No, not another woman my little Wufferly-Pufferly. I've met a ray-bee.

**Harris**    A rabbi, Sir.

**Clarissa**    But isn't that some kind of holy man?

**Dominic**    You are exactly right old thing. He is indeed a holy man. He used to be a carpenter but now he goes about healing people and preaching and ... and being holy. Jolly exciting, what!

| | |
|---|---|
| **Harris** | Would I be correct in presuming that the holy gentleman to whom you are referring is Mr Jesus of Nazareth? |
| **Dominic** | You've heard of him. |
| **Harris** | Yes Sir. The gentleman seems to have raised a few eyebrows. |
| **Dominic** | How so? |
| **Harris** | He advocates a personal salvation scheme based on a personal knowledge of himself. |
| **Dominic** | Does he, by Jove? |
| **Harris** | It is deemed somewhat controversial by the religious establishment. |
| **Dominic** | Oh. Well I met him earlier today and I asked him what I must do to inherit eternal life. |
| **Clarissa** | What did he say? |
| **Dominic** | Keep the commandments. |
| **Nanny** | You already do that. You were brought up to be a good boy. |
| **Clarissa** | Is that all? |
| **Dominic** | Just about. Apart from selling everything and giving the proceeds to the poor, and then simply following him. |
| **Nanny** | Oh, that's interesting, dear. |
| **Dominic** | Yes. From now on it's a life on the open road for me. And for you since I know you'll all be keen to join me. |
| **Harris** | Join you, Sir? |
| **Dominic** | Of course, I'm going to become a disciple of Mr Jesus. I'm going to give up everything and put my faith in him. |
| **Clarissa** | When you say "give up everything", what exactly do you mean? |
| **Dominic** | The business, the estate, the cars, you know, all the unimportant things in life. |

| | |
|---|---|
| **Clarissa** | And you want us to join you? |
| **Dominic** | It'll be a real wheeze. Open air, good companions, doing good, and of course, eternal life. I want all of you to come along and share in it. Lend a hand and what have you. |
| **Harris** | Will this be a salaried position, Sir? |
| **Dominic** | Money isn't the issue, Harris. |
| **Harris** | That may be the case, Sir, but it's absence does give rise to certain difficulties. |
| **Dominic** | How so? |
| **Harris** | The one that immediately springs to mind, Sir, is how precisely, without the prerequisite financial facilities, do you plan to retain my services? |
| **Clarissa** | And how can you possibly expect to keep me in the manner to which I've become accustomed? |
| **Nanny** | And all that fresh air is only going to bring on your chest problem again. Especially if you don't keep warm at night. |
| **Harris** | If I may be so bold as to make a suggestion, Sir? |
| **Dominic** | Er ... yes. Fire away. |
| **Harris** | Contact Mr Jesus and ask if you can negotiate for eternal life on more favourable terms. |
| **Nanny** | Oh now that is a sensible idea. |
| **Clarissa** | After all, giving up everything for this Jesus fellow is all very well, but you have such an awful lot to give up. Me, for example. |
| **Dominic** | I have rather, haven't I. |
| **Nanny** | Why don't you tell him about your chest, I'm sure he'll understand you need to be kept comfortable. |

**Harris**   Explain to him that you were not raised in a manner that prepared you for a life of sacrifice. Tell him you will be happy to make regular donations to a charity of his choice.

**Clarissa**   Make him understand that you have responsibilities. Say you'll be happy to give up one day a week for him. Sunday's good. Most of the shops are shut.

**Dominic**   Yes, right. Perhaps I ought to talk to him.

**All**   Yes.

**Dominic**   Right. Let me see ... ( *He takes out a mobile phone.* ) He's on Bethany 178. It's ringing ... Hello? Martha, is Jesus there? Lord? Hello, it's me, Dominic. I'm very well, thank you. Now about this eternal life thing. How much would you say it was really worth?

**END**

# The Witness for the Prosecution
## Bible background
*John 13.36-38, John 18.15-18, 25-27.*

My name is Tamar. I'm a servant in the house of Caiaphas.

I was carrying sticks from the woodpile to the fire. It was cool that night, cold even. A few minutes earlier soldiers had brought Jesus into the house. After they had passed through and things had quietened down I saw Simon Peter slip quietly into the courtyard.

Anyone could have seen his distress. Caiaphas was no friend of Jesus, nor of any associated with him. If they could come at night and try the Nazarene, then the rule of law had been put aside, at least on this occasion.

I recognised Simon Peter, as would half of Jerusalem at that time. For wherever Jesus was, he was there, loud and assured. He seemed so proud that Jesus had chosen him. I heard later than when Jesus was arrested Simon Peter defended him with a sword. That was easy to believe. Yes, I recognised him, he had a certain notoriety. I was young and he was attractive.

By this time several people had gathered around the fire, and when I added wood to its flames I spoke to Simon Peter. I wanted to know what was happening. 'You were with Jesus of Galilee,' I said to him. But he denied it. He said he didn't know what I was talking about. He stood up and walked to the gates of the courtyard. I could see he was shaking.

Naomi, another servant, told those around the fire that she was sure he had been with Jesus. Simon Peter heard her and although he swore before us all that he didn't know him, it was his eyes: his eyes betrayed him.

Eventually one of the men called out loudly that he knew he was a follower of the rabbi from Galilee - his accent had given him away. And then in Peter's face I saw panic. There were soldiers all around.

'I swear I'm telling the truth!' he shouted. Everyone turned and looked. 'May God punish me if I am not! I do not know the man!'

At that moment a cock crowed, and for a few seconds there was only silence. Then the soldiers led Jesus from the house. He looked over to where Peter was standing. And in that moment, as they saw each other, caught in the light of the fire, I could see the tears on Peter's face.

Then Peter turned and fled.

**END**

# Thieves Paradise

## Characters

*Joseph*

*Jack*

## Bible background

*Luke 23.32-43*

*The sketch takes place in the bar of the local pub. The two characters may be drinking from beer glasses.*

| | |
|---|---|
| **Joseph** | It near broke my heart to see old Barney hanging there. |
| **Jack** | Hanging where? |
| **Joseph** | On a big wooden cross. |
| **Jack** | So why was he doing that? |
| **Joseph** | Well mostly because of the nails. |
| **Jack** | What, real nails? |
| **Joseph** | Yes. |
| **Jack** | That's a bit barbaric. You could kill someone like that. |
| **Joseph** | They did. Barney, Jim and that Jesus. |
| **Jack** | So Barney's dead is he? |
| **Joseph** | Yeah, he was crucified. |
| **Jack** | Nasty. |
| **Joseph** | He was a good bloke. |
| **Jack** | Well, he wasn't that good. He was a thief. That's why they crucified him I expect. |
| **Joseph** | Yes, but he was a good thief. |
| **Jack** | No he wasn't. He got caught. |

| | |
|---|---|
| **Joseph** | He never had any luck. |
| **Jack** | No. |
| **Joseph** | Fancy breaking into a geezer's house when you absolutely positively know he's not going to be there, and then being caught in the act when he comes home totally unexpected. |
| **Jack** | Yeah. What was that bloke's name again? |
| **Joseph** | Lazarus. |
| **Jack** | Chance in a million that. |
| **Joseph** | Yeah. Poor old Barney. |
| **Jack** | Mind you, Jim wasn't much better. I mean, fancy breaking into a house only to find the owner had given everything away. |
| **Joseph** | Blooming Zacchaeus. |
| **Jack** | And fancy both of them breaking into that gate keeper's house ... |
| **Joseph** | ... only to be spotted by an eyewitness. |
| **Both** | Blind Bartimaeus. |
| **Joseph** | Still, in their line of work they knew they were taking a risk. |
| **Jack** | What about that other bloke? |
| **Joseph** | Who, Jesus? |
| **Jack** | What was his crime? |
| **Joseph** | It was funny that. No one seemed to know. |
| **Jack** | What was he? A thief? Con man? Fraudster? Mugger? |
| **Joseph** | Rabbi. |
| **Jack** | What, a holy man? |

| | |
|---|---|
| **Joseph** | Apparently. He had a sign on his cross saying he was the king of the Jews. But I heard people saying that he was the son of God. |
| **Jack** | If he was the son of God, what was he doing nailed to a cross? |
| **Joseph** | That's what Jim said. He gave him a really hard time, mocking him and shouting at him to save himself and them. |
| **Jack** | Jim was a hard man. |
| **Joseph** | As hard as nails. |
| **Jack** | Not quite ... What about Barney? |
| **Joseph** | Barney was a bit different. He seemed to recognise something in Jesus. |
| **Jack** | It's a pity he didn't meet him earlier. He might not have ended up where he did. |
| **Joseph** | They seemed to get on well enough though, given the circumstances. |
| **Jack** | How do you mean? |
| **Joseph** | I heard Barney ask if Jesus would remember him when he came into his kingdom. |
| **Jack** | As if Jesus didn't have enough on his plate. |
| **Joseph** | That's what I thought. But Jesus made him this promise, see? |
| **Jack** | What kind of promise can you make to a dying man? |
| **Joseph** | He said, "I tell you the truth, today you will be with me in paradise". |
| **Jack** | What do you think he meant by that? |
| **Joseph** | That he was for ... for ... for ... |
| **Jack** | ... four sheets to the wind? |
| **Joseph** | No, that he was for ... for ... for ... |

| | |
|---|---|
| **Jack** | ... for he's a jolly good fellow? |
| **Joseph** | No, that he was for ... for ... for ... |
| **Jack** | ... fortunate? |
| **Joseph** | Hardly. No, that he was forgiven. |
| **Jack** | Oh. |
| **Joseph** | Yeah, nice thought that. |
| **Jack** | Anyway, I'm going to miss old Barney. |
| **Joseph** | Yeah, but at least his suffering is over. |
| **Jack** | Was that Jesus the same bloke who's been preaching all over the place? |
| **Joseph** | I suppose so, yeah. |
| **Jack** | I heard him once. |
| **Joseph** | Oh yeah? |
| **Jack** | I hope that when he made him that promise he knew what Barney's profession was. |
| **Joseph** | What do you mean? A housebreaker? Well what does that matter now? |
| **Jack** | Because it was Jesus who said, "in my father's house are many mansions." |
| **Joseph** | Then Barney really will be in paradise. |

**END**

# Stephen

## Bible background
*Acts 7.54 - 60*

**A**     I watched them drag Stephen from the city.

**B**     They took him to die.

**C**     Yelling, we stoned him.

**A**     Screaming, I begged them to stop.

**D**     Patiently, I waited for it all to be over.

**B**     I heard him say

**C**     Look!

**A**     And he lifted his head.

**C**     I see heaven open and the Son of Man standing at the right hand of God.

**B**     We covered our ears against such words.

**A**     Such a vision!

**D**     Such blasphemy!

**A**     Such certainty.

**C**     So we took him to a place outside the city.

**D**     There they laid cloaks at my feet.

**B**     And we took up stones and hurled them.

**C**     Mine hit him here, on the upper arm.

**A**     I saw him flinch.

**D**     Stephen prayed ...

**C**     Lord Jesus receive my spirit.

**A**     He fell to his knees.

**B**      Stones rained on him.

**A**      He cried out ...

**C**      Lord do not hold this sin against them.

**A**      And then he fell asleep.

**B**      But I saw it on his face. There was a deeper joy.

**C**      He showed no fear ... although he must have known pain.

**D**      And later, during my own times of suffering, I remembered his words.

**C**      The Son of Man standing at the right hand of God.

**A**      He lit a flame of witness, which has been passed on ... one to one.

**B**      He has received the promise of God and it has carried him home.

**END**

# Spies R Us

## Characters

*Spies 1 - 4*
*Woman*

### Bible background
Luke 19.1-10

*This sketch has five speaking parts and room for any number of additional Mr X's. Spy 1 enters and knocks on a door. The door is opened by a woman.*

**Spy 1**      The pickled cow is already blue.

**Woman**      What?

**Spy 1**      The pickled cow is already blue.

**Woman**      If you say so, dear, but I think you've got the wrong address.

**Spy 1**      Oh. I'm looking for the spies and undercover guild (Jerusalem chapter).

**Woman**      Oh them! They're meeting next door. Another secret get together is it?

**Spy 1**      Yes ... I mean no. I mean maybe.

**Woman**      Well you just tell them to keep the noise down this time. These walls are paper-thin.

**Spy 1**      Right. Ta, I mean thank you.

*Spy 1 knocks on another door. The door is opened by spy 2.*

**Spy 1**      The pickled cow is already blue.

**Spy 2**      And the red herring is best eaten with custard.

**Spy 1**      Thank goodness.

| | |
|---|---|
| **Spy 2** | Quick, come in. We don't want the neighbours to suspect anything. |
| **Spy 1** | No, of course not. |
| **Spy 2** | Let me introduce you to everyone. I'm Mr X and over there is Mr X. Next to him is Mr X and on his right is Mr X. That's Mr X, Mr X, and Mr X, on the settee. And that's Mr X in the corner. |
| **Spy 1** | Where? Behind the potted plant? |
| **Spy 2** | No, disguised as the potted plant. |
| **Spy 1** | That's amazing. |
| **Spy 2** | And your name is? |
| **Spy 1** | Mr X. No relation. |
| **Spy 2** | Good to meet you. Well I think everyone is here now. So let's get under way. X, could you read the minutes of the last meeting? |
| **Spy 3** | Glib sprottle glob. Mip sly blip mootle mar gleep. Plitch. |
| **Spy 2** | Yes, perhaps you could decode them first. |
| **Spy 3** | Spittle. I mean sorry. |
| **Spy 2** | We'll come back to those later. Now this meeting has been convened to discuss the Nazarene file. |
| **Spy 4** | What, again? |
| **Spy 2** | The matter hasn't been dealt with to anyone's satisfaction as yet. |
| **Spy 4** | How can one carpenter cause so much trouble? |
| **Spy 1** | But I thought he was supposed to be dead. |
| **Spy 2** | He is. |
| **Spy 1** | Then what's the problem? |

| | |
|---|---|
| **Spy 2** | He didn't stay that way. |
| **Spy 1** | How can you not stay dead? |
| **Spy 2** | He got better. |
| **Spy 1** | You mean to say he's found a cure for death? |
| **Spy 2** | The evidence does seem to point in that direction, yes. |
| **Spy 4** | Unreasonable behaviour, that's what he's displaying. Rising from the dead, I mean, it's not natural. |
| **Spy 2** | Maybe. But it's not actually illegal either. Inconvenient, yes. Inconsiderate, certainly. But resurrection is not technically an offence. The man's been tried, found guilty, and executed once already. It would be embarrassing to go through it all again. Now, any thoughts on the matter? Yes, X? |
| **Spy 3** | Ten plinkle fitch? |
| **Spy 2** | That's a good point, but I'm afraid there are too many witnesses that have seen him up and about. They can't all be hallucinating. |
| **Spy 1** | You are sure he was actually dead? I mean, he might just have been pretending to die. |
| **Spy 2** | I oversaw the execution myself, on behalf of our paymasters, the Sanhedrin. The subject was dead within six hours of being nailed to that cross. It was a neat, professional job. |
| **Spy 4** | Have we made any progress in discovering who this man really was? |
| **Spy 2** | That's the burning question. If we knew who this Jesus Davidson really was we could take the appropriate action. |
| **Spy 1** | Supposing he really is the son of God? |
| **Spy 2** | Don't be ridiculous. |
| **Spy 1** | Well that's what people are saying. |
| **Spy 2** | Are they indeed? |

| | |
|---|---|
| **Spy 1** | Yes. |
| **Spy 2** | Well  I think it's time we took decisive action. I'm assigning special agent Saul of Tarsus to the case.  He'll sort these people out. |
| **Spy 4** | He's a bit extreme, isn't he? |
| **Spy 2** | He'll get the job done. I can't see him going around letting people say that Jesus is the son of God. Yes, Saul of Tarsus is the man we need. I know exactly where to send him. Anybody got a map of Damascus? |

**END**

# The Five Minute Bible
## Characters
*A, B, C and D*

*This sketch is like no other. It must be delivered very fast from the start and get faster towards the end of the Old Testament section before a very brief pause leading into the New Testament section. The humour comes from the pace of delivery rather than the actual words. The four actors should rarely stop moving so the overall effect is a blur of words and action.*

**A**     Ladies and gentlemen, we present to you ...

**B**     ... The Bible ...

**C**     In just five minutes.

**D**     Genesis.

**A**     In the beginning God created the heavens and the earth.

**B**     It took him just seven days.

**A**     Which is pretty quick to build anything. Just ask the men who fitted my kitchen cupboards.

**C**     The pinnacle of his creation was Man.

**D**     Specifically a man called Adam.

**B**     Who was quickly joined by a woman called Eve.

**A**     So far so good.

**B**     But ...

**D**     ... Eve was tempted by a serpent to eat from the tree of forbidden knowledge.

**C**     A serious mistake on her part.

**B**  Which had a knock on effect on Adam because sin had entered the world.

**D**  And shattered the relationship between man and God.

**A**  Adam and Eve had two sons called Cain and Abel.

*B (Cain) kills D (Abel).*

**C**  As you can see, the human race is off to a good start

**A**  Where is your brother?

**B**  Am I my brother's keeper?

**D**  Things went from bad to ... well ... badder.

**C**  And God decided to wipe the slate clean and start again.

**A**  Noah.

**B**  The planet's one good man.

**A**  Was told to build an ark and rescue some livestock.

**C**  It rained and rained for forty days and forty nights.

**B**  Which had a detrimental effect on the environment.

**C**  So everybody and everything drowned.

**D**  Except those aboard Noah's ark.

**A**  God promised he wouldn't destroy his creation again and as a sign of this covenant he gave us the ...

**B**  ... Rainbow.

**D**  Rushing on.

**C**  Because we're still only in Genesis.

**A** The descendants of Noah built the tower of Babel, which was the Canary Wharf of its day.

**D** It brought about the division of nations.

**B** Eventually Abraham came on the scene.

**C** He became the father of the children of Israel.

**A** Soon came Jacob who wrestled with angels and dreamed of a ladder up to heaven.

**B** He had many sons who became the tribes of Israel.

**C** One of the sons was Joseph, who went on to star in a hugely successful West End musical and who strangely had an Australian accent.

**D** *(Sings)* I closed my eyes, drew back the curtains, and saw for certain, any dream will do.

**A** No you didn't, we don't have time.

**B** Joseph and his brothers ended up in Egypt.

**C** But they outstayed their welcome and eventually ended up as slaves.

**D** Which brings us to the book of Exodus. How are we doing for time?

**A** Badly. We'll have to speed up. Ready?

**B,C,D** Ready.

**A** Moses met God in the desert.

**B** He was disguised as a burning bush.

**A** God that is, not Moses.

**D** God told Moses to free his people from slavery.

**C** Moses went to see Pharaoh who laughed in his face.

**A**  So Moses and God came up with a plan.

**B**  God visited upon Egypt a series of plagues, culminating in the death of the first born children.

**C**  After which, Pharaoh was only too pleased to see the back of Moses and the children of Israel.

**D**  So off they set, into the wilderness.

**A**  But before they could get very far Pharaoh changed his mind and sent his army to bring them back.

**B**  Moses found himself trapped between the Red Sea and a fearsome army.

**D**  What could he do?

**A**  Stand and fight?

**B**  Or run and drown?

**C**  A tricky choice.

**D**  Fortunately there was a third option.

**B**  Run and not drown.

**A**  Yes folks, Moses parted the Red sea and the children of Israel escaped.

**C**  While the Egyptian army was washed away like a stain in a Daz Ultra commercial.

**B**  The children of Israel wandered for forty years around the wilderness.

**D**  They were given the Ten Commandments and they finally made it into the promised land.

**A**  All bar Moses who died before reaching it.

**C**  Now the books of Leviticus, Numbers and Deuteronomy.

**B**     Lots of laws.

**A**     And some battles.

**C**     Then the book of Joshua.

**A,B,D** *(Sings)*
Joshua fought the battle of Jericho, Jericho, Jericho.
Joshua fought the battle of Jericho,
and the walls came tumbling down.

**C**     And on to Judges.

**A**     A book that paints pictures of its heroes, warts and all.

**D**     Deborah, a gifted lady.

**B**     Barak, unwilling to take on responsibility.

**C**     Gideon, started out as a coward, became a remarkable military strategist, and then tailed off as an idol worshipper.

**A**     Jephthah, a brave soldier who didn't always think before he opened his big mouth.

**B**     *(As Jephthah)* Lord, if you help me win this battle I will sacrifice to you as a burnt offering whatever comes out of my door when I get home.

**D**     Nice thought, Jeph, but haven't you forgotten that you live with your only daughter?

**B**     *(As Jephthah)* Oops!

**C**     And of course there was good old Sampson and the most expensive haircut in history.

**A**     Which brings us to the end of Judges and on to Ruth.

**B**     A book about love and loyalty against a background of violence and racism.

**A**   Then on to 1 Samuel and 2 Samuel.

**D**   Which might better be called the Book of David.

**B**   Samuel was Israel's first king but David was her greatest.

**A**   In his youth David fought the mighty Goliath.

> *There is a very quick enactment of the David and Goliath battle.*

**C**   Then David spent some time as an outlaw.

**D**   But when Saul died David succeeded him.

**B**   He fought many battles and had an affair with Bathsheba.

**A**   He also had a major problem with one of his sons, Absalom.

**D**   All in all a fairly typical royal family saga.

**C**   Now on to Kings 1 and 2.

**B**   The golden age of Israel. The reign of King Solomon.

**A**   Solomon was very wise because he nearly chopped a baby in half.

**C**   Solomon was a great King because he built the great temple.

**D**   Solomon had a great sex life. He had seven hundred wives and three hundred concubines.

**B**   But his wives led him astray and he started to build temples for false gods.

**A**   So after his death the country fell apart and eventually was invaded by the Babylonians.

**C**   The temple was destroyed.

**B**   And the children of Israel were taken into exile.

**D**   The books of 1 and 2 Chronicles cover the same ground and ...

**A**  ... Ezra, Nehemiah and Esther cover the period in exile in Babylon and the return of the people to Israel ...

**B**  ... and the rebuilding of the temple.

**C**  Interestingly, Esther is the only book in the Bible not to actually mention God.

**D**  Now come the Wisdom books.

**A**  Job, a story of steadfast faith in the face of great suffering.

**B**  Psalms, 150 hymns, prayers and poems covering the full range of human emotion.

**C**  Proverbs, lots of wisdom.

**D**  Ecclesiastes, lots more wisdom.

**A**  Song of Songs, lots of sex.

**B**  Then come the books of the prophets.

**D**  The general theme of which is, "turn back to the Lord, O Israel".

**C**  Isaiah and Jeremiah.

**A**  Lamentations, author unknown, very sad.

**D**  Ezekiel.

**C**  Daniel, famed for his exploits with lions.

**B**  Then Hosea, Joel, Amos and Obadiah.

**A**  Jonah, swallowed by a great fish and then thrown up in Nineveh.

**B**  Micah, Nahum, Habakkuk.

**C**  Zephaniah, Haggai.

**D**  Zechariah and Malachi.

**A**      Which brings us, exhausted, to the end of the Old Testament.

*All four actors pause briefly and recover their breaths.*

**B**      The New Testament.

**A,C,D** Right.

**B**      The New Testament starts with the Gospels.

**A**      Meaning the good news.

**C**      Mathew, Mark, Luke and John.

**D**      The books about Jesus.

**B**      Jesus was born of the virgin Mary, in a stable in Bethlehem.

**C**      He was baptised by his cousin John the Baptist.

**A**      Then he spent three years teaching and healing throughout the land.

**B**      During this time he ...

**C**      ... turned water into wine.

**D**      Walked on water.

**A**      Fed over five thousand people with just two loaves and five fish.

**C**      Raised Lazarus from the dead.

**D**      Healed the sick.

**B**      Told many stories.

**C**      Upset the Pharisees.

**A**      Upset the money lenders.

**B**      But he never sinned.

**C**      He never turned his back on anyone.

**D**      And he never deserved to die.

**A**      A plot was hatched against him.

**D**      He broke the bread and he poured out the wine.

**B**      A friend ...

**C**      ... Judas ...

**B**      ... betrayed him.

**C**      He was taken before Pilate and tried.

**A**      And although he was innocent he was found guilty and sentenced to die.

**B**      Crucified.

**D**      On a hill outside the city.

> *One of the actors strikes a crucifixion pose. This is held for a few seconds.*

**C**      They buried him in a tomb sealed with a large rock.

**A**      But on the third day he rose from the dead.

**B**      And was seen by many people.

**C**      He told his friend Peter to feed his lambs.

**D**      Then comes the Acts of the Apostles.

**A**      Jesus ascends to heaven.

**C**      The Holy Spirit descends like tongues of fire.

**B**      And the church is born.

**D**      Stephen is stoned to death. The first Christian martyr.

**A**      Saul sees a blinding light on the road to Damascus.

**B**     He changes his name to Paul and becomes a great Christian missionary.

**C**     Paul and others write many letters of encouragement and teaching.

**D**     Romans.

**A**     One Corinthians, two Corinthians, Galatians, Ephesians.

**B**     Phillipians, Colossians, Thessalonians one and two.

**C**     One Timothy, two Timothy, Titus and Philemon.

**D**     Hebrews, James.

**B**     Peter, Peter, John, John, John.

**C**     Jude.

**D**     But the final book of the Bible is not a letter but rather a vision.

**A**     The end of this world and the beginning of a new world.

**B**     Of Jesus come in glory.

**C**     The Revelation of Saint John the Divine.

**D**     The Bible ends thus.

**A**     He who testifies to these things says ...

**C**     Yes, I am coming soon.

**D**     Amen.

**B**     Come Lord Jesus.

**A**     The grace of the Lord Jesus be with God's people.

**ALL** Amen.


**END**

# The Book Of Fish

## Characters

*Ernest*

*John*

*John is sat on a park bench reading his Bible and eating a packed lunch. Enter Ernest. He sits down next to John.*

**Ernest**   You don't mind if I sit here, do you?

**John**   No, not at all.

**Ernest**   Only I wouldn't want to disturb you.

**John**   Thank you.

**Ernest**   I can see that you are reading. I hate it when people disturb me when I'm reading. I find that most annoying ... That's very irritating when people interrupt me when I'm reading a good book ... Are you reading a good book?

**John**   The Bible.

**Ernest**   Not so much a good book as the Good Book. Ha ha. Just my little joke. Well then I really mustn't disturb you. I don't want to be struck by lightning! Ha ha.

**John**   Thank you.

*They sit in silence. John continues to read. Ernest starts to read over John's shoulder.*

**Ernest**   Good is it? The Good Book?

**John**   Yes.

**Ernest**   I've read a lot of books myself. There's nothing I like better than a good book. Not the Good Book you understand. Any good book. Personally I don't think the Bible is a very good book. I find it very over rated.

| | |
|---|---|
| **John** | I'm sorry you feel that way. I find it very helpful. |
| **Ernest** | Helpful! I've never found it helpful. Take for example the subject of goldfish. |
| **John** | Goldfish? |
| **Ernest** | Fascinating creatures, I think you'll agree. Did you know that the goldfish has the widest range of vision of any known creature? It can see all the way from infrared to ultraviolet. I read that in a book. But that book was not the Bible. |
| **John** | Really? |
| **Ernest** | You won't read about goldfish in the Bible, did you know that? |
| **John** | No. |
| **Ernest** | The Bible is silent on the subject of goldfish. Goldfish are not deemed worthy of inclusion in the holy canon. You can scan the entire contents from cover to cover and not a word will you find pertaining to the common goldfish. I find that strange. After all, if the bible is the true word of God then you would have thought that goldfish would feature somewhere in it. They are, after all, supposed to be part of his creation. No, if you want to read about the real world you won't read about it in the Bible. You won't learn that the goldfish is a member of the carp family by reading the Bible. *Genus Carassius* will remain a mystery to you. |
| **John** | I suppose it will. |
| **Ernest** | And that, if you don't mind me saying, is the big problem with the Bible. |
| **John** | What, that it doesn't mention goldfish? |
| **Ernest** | No, that it's just not relevant to the way we live our lives today. I want a book that tells me things I want to know about. |
| **John** | Are we still talking about goldfish? |

| | |
|---|---|
| **Ernest** | I believe you will find no mention of pandas in the scriptures. Nor even the kangaroo. Electricity doesn't get a look in. Neither does Japan. In fact I dare say I could go on to mention many more things that the Bible fails to take account of. The planet Neptune for example. |
| **John** | I'm sorry but I really don't understand your point. |
| **Ernest** | My point is that people say the Bible contains answers. I have looked into the Bible many times in search of answers and I have never found them. When, for example, I wanted to find the answer to the question "what is the capital of Nicaragua?" I was completely let down by the Bible. |
| **John** | Managua. |
| **Ernest** | Pardon? |
| **John** | The capital of Nicaragua is Managua. |
| **Ernest** | Is it? Thank you. But you didn't learn that from the Bible, did you? |
| **John** | No, from my geography teacher. |
| **Ernest** | Time and time again I've looked in the Bible for answers and I haven't found them. |
| **John** | Have you looked for answers that don't directly relate to goldfish? |
| **Ernest** | Are you suggesting that the Bible doesn't have the answers to all life's questions? Because if you are then you are severely out of step with traditional church teachings. |
| **John** | I don't know if the Bible has the answer to all life's questions but it does have the answer to some of the biggest ones. It tells us about how God loves us and how we can know him. It's full of poetry and parables, history and biographies, letters, laws, and proverbs. |

| | |
|---|---|
| **Ernest** | But no fish. |
| **John** | It's full of fish! Big fish, fish with coins in their mouths, fish in nets, fish served with bread al fresco, and even fishers of men. |
| **Ernest** | But none of them gold in colour. |
| **John** | It doesn't specify colour. |
| **Ernest** | So some of them might actually be gold. |
| **John** | Well ... I suppose that might be so. |
| **Ernest** | I may have to reassess my evaluation of the Bible. It may have more relevance than I had previously believed. It might even be able to help me with the answers I seek. Answers I have sought for years. |

*John stands up to leave.  He hands Ernest the Bible.*

| | |
|---|---|
| **John** | I have to leave now. Please keep this and read it. Perhaps it can help. |
| **Ernest** | Thank you. |
| **John** | Goodbye. |

*Exit John.  Ernest opens up the Bible.*

| | |
|---|---|
| **Ernest** | You never know. It might just be possible ... Now where would I find the book of Jonah? |

**END**

# About the Author

**Stephen Deal** was a founder member of **Stripes Theatre Company** in 1986 and toured extensively until 1994. As the company's principal writer he wrote several revues. His play *Judas* was performed at the 1986 Edinburgh Festival 'Fringe'. The show *Pilgrims* was performed at over fifty venues in 1990 and 1991. *Gospel End* (1992 with Rob Frost) was seen throughout the U.K. The revue *Burning Questions* (written with Paul Field) was recorded for a CD (available from Kingsway) in 1993 and toured nationally in 1994. In 1996, an open air theatre event, *Jubilate!* (with music by Rick Wakeman) was seen in 27 towns and combined a professional cast with local actors.

In early 1999 the show *Hopes and Dreams*, for which Stephen wrote the drama and two performance poems, was a sell out at over 35 major venues. (The Script, CD and Score are available from Kingsway). The show also spawned the Platinum selling number one hit single 'The Millennium Prayer' for Sir Cliff Richard and earned Stephen (and Paul Field) prestigious Ivor Novello awards.

Stephen has also written material for television and radio and his sketches appear in numerous publications. In recent years he has co-founded **The Quick Sketch Theatre Company** and has taken to occasional public speaking. He regularly appears at the large Christian event *Easter People*. In 2002 he once again teamed up with Rob Frost and Paul Field to co-write *Hear and Now*, a show based on the Sermon on the Mount.

He is married to Polly, and together with their son Matthew, they live in Surrey, 'behind a duck pond'. His hobbies include an interest in Magic and collecting useless bits of information.

**Stephen's web site is: http://www.stephendeal.org
and he welcomes emails at stephen@stephendeal.org.
His books are available from any Christian bookshop,
Amazon.co.uk or directly from his publisher.**